SHERIDAN SCHOOL
1201 University Ave. NE
Minneapolis, MN 55413

PERFECTION LEARNING®

Scaly and Scary

Helen Lepp Friesen

Table of Contents

1. A Cold-Blooded Reptile 3
2. In the Water and on Land 6
3. From Egg to Gator 8
4. An Alligator's Wardrobe 12
5. A-Hunting We Will Go 14
   Glossary 16

Chapter 1
A Cold-Blooded Reptile

Alligators are cold-blooded reptiles. That does not mean that they have cold blood. It just means that they do not turn food energy into heat. Their inside temperature is the same as the temperature around them.

Alligators bask in the sun when they are too cold.

4

When they are hot, they move to the shade or into the water. That is why they live in warm, moist climates near lakes, rivers, and swamps.

Chapter 2
In the Water and on Land

Alligators spend their time in the water and on land. Their eyes, ears, and nose are high on their head.

Their nostrils are near the tip of the snout. That way they can still breathe air when they are mostly in water.

Chapter 3
From Egg to Gator

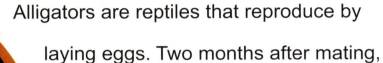

Alligators are reptiles that reproduce by laying eggs. Two months after mating, the mother alligator lays around 30 to 50 eggs.

She makes a pile of leaves, grass, and dirt. Then she digs a hole in the pile for her eggs. She covers the eggs with leaves and mud. While she waits for the eggs to hatch, she digs a pool nearby.

Young alligators use an egg tooth on their snout to break out of their shell. When the mother hears the babies squeak, she digs them out.

She carries them to the pool in her mouth.

The young alligators look for food there. They eat water plants, shrimp, crawfish, or crabs.

Chapter 4

An Alligator's Wardrobe

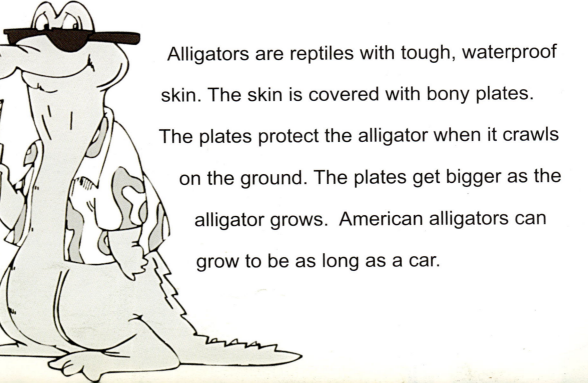

Alligators are reptiles with tough, waterproof skin. The skin is covered with bony plates. The plates protect the alligator when it crawls on the ground. The plates get bigger as the alligator grows. American alligators can grow to be as long as a car.

On land, alligators look lazy. If they are frightened, they can run fast on their short, stubby legs. They have webbed feet with claws.

Webbed feet with claws

Alligator plates

Chapter 5

A-Hunting We Will Go

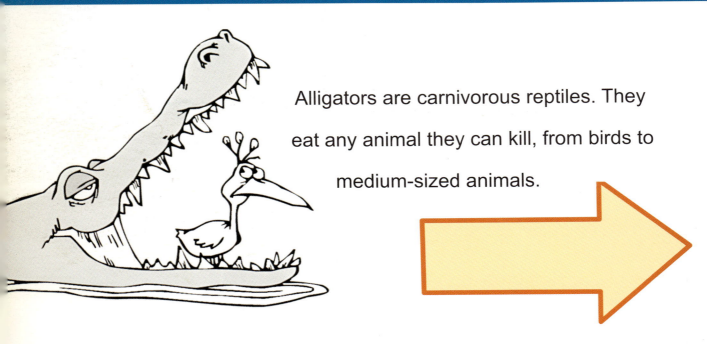

Alligators are carnivorous reptiles. They eat any animal they can kill, from birds to medium-sized animals.

That's a Lot of Alligators!

It is thought that more than 1 million wild alligators live in Florida!

They wait quietly in the weeds. When a duck, fish, rabbit, or other animal comes close, they grab it.

Glossary

Alligator eggs

Alligator nest

Bony plates

Egg tooth

Short, stubby legs

Webbed feet

Leveled content-area science books in Earth/Space Science, Life Science, Math in Science, Physical Science, Science and Technology, and Science as Inquiry for emergent, early, and fluent readers

Scaly and Scary
Written by Helen Lepp Friesen

Text © 2006 by Perfection Learning® Corporation

All rights reserved. No part of this book may be reproduced, stored in a retrieval system, or transmitted in any form or by any means, electronic, mechanical, photocopying, recording, or otherwise, without prior permission of the publisher.

Printed in the United States of America.

For information, contact

Perfection Learning® Corporation

1000 North Second Avenue, P.O. Box 500
Logan, Iowa 51546-0500.
Phone: 1-800-831-4190
Fax: 1-800-543-2745

perfectionlearning.com

PB ISBN-13: 978-0-7891-6715-6
PB ISBN-10: 0-7891-6715-8

2 3 4 5 6 7 RD 12 11 10 09 08 07

Book design: Melissa Leeds

Image credits:

Photos.com: cover, pp. 1, 4, 5, 7;
©Royalty-Free/Corbis: pp. 3, 6, 13;
istock photos: back cover, pp. 2, 13, 16, 15, 16;
clipart.com: pp. 3, 4, 7, 10, 11, 12, 14, 15;
Kent A. Vilet: pp. 8, 9, 10, 11, 16